ONE LESS
GRAIN OF SAND

Make a Difference
While You Have Time

30-Day Devotional

Joey A. Perry, Sr.

Albatross Publishing
Tomball, Texas 77377

https://joeyaperry.com

*This book is dedicated to God the Father,
Who loves and sustains me, Jesus Christ the
Son, Who died and was resurrected so I can
have eternal life, and the Holy Spirit,
Who indwells and empowers me.*

Acknowledgments

*F*irst and foremost, I thank God for giving me the inspiration and ability to write this devotional and the discipline to complete it. God can use anyone He desires to accomplish His work, so I never take it for granted when He chooses to use me.

Even though my name is on the cover, this book would not be what it is without the assistance of several other people. I thank my amazing wife, Vanessa, for her support and encouragement as I wrote. She was a great sounding board and provided invaluable feedback on the book's contents and cover design.

I thank the following people for reviewing this work and giving me their comments, recommendations, and suggestions: Vanessa, Rev. Lawrence Brewster, Max Burton, Leatha Moore, and Robert Riley. All of these individuals are strong believers in God, are well-versed in the Bible, and are committed servants of Jesus Christ. I am extremely grateful to them for sacrificing their time to help make this book the best that it could be for the Lord.

I thank Linda Stubblefield for editing the manuscript, fixing my grammatical errors, and helping to give the book a professional look and feel.

FREE PRINTABLE JOURNAL

*I*n addition to being a devotional, this book is also a journal. Each daily reading includes questions or statements for personal reflection. To make it easier for eBook readers to respond to the journal prompts, **a free downloadable and printable journal is available**. Print book readers can also use the downloadable journal if they choose not to write their responses directly in their book.

To access the journal, visit the web address shown below.

https://joeyaperry.com/free-journal-volume-2/

SHARE A PRAYER

Several journal prompts in this book ask you to write a prayer related to that day's devotion. **While it is true that your prayers can be extremely personal, there are times when your prayers can be shared with others and may be just what they need to hear at that moment in their lives.**

The focus of this book is to make a difference in the world. **One way you can make a difference is by inspiring other believers through your prayers.** The prayers you utter for yourself can strengthen and bless others who hear them. **As you write prayers in response to the journal prompts, please consider sharing some of those prayers with others.** If a devotion causes you to say a prayer that is not in response to a journal prompt, feel free to share that prayer also.

To share your prayers, go to the link below, enter your prayer in the comment field, and click the submit button. Thank you for your prayers!

https://joeyaperry.com/share-a-prayer/

Introduction

"**All good things must come to an end.**" We see the truth of this expression in the fact that influential leaders pass away, great athletes retire, and successful company presidents step down. From an individual perspective, at some point, all of our lives on this earth will be over, either when we die or when Jesus Christ returns. James 4:14 declares, *"Why, you do not even know what will happen tomorrow. What is your life? You are a mist that appears for a little while and then vanishes."* **Given the inevitability that your life will end one day, what will you do to make a difference in the world before God tells you your time is up?**

In my previous book, *One Less Grain of Sand: Fulfill God's Purposes While You Have Time!*, I said life can be represented by an hourglass. In this analogy, the sand in the bottom of the hourglass represents the time we have lived, whereas the sand in the top represents the time we have left. **With every second we live, a grain of sand drops from the top to the bottom of our hourglass, so there is "one less grain of sand," or a little less time, remaining in our life.** That 30-day devotional focuses on encouraging us to live for God and fulfill His purposes while we are still alive. Once that last grain of sand drops, our life will be over and we will be unable to do anything else on this side of heaven.

One Less Grain of Sand: Make a Difference While You Have Time follows the same idea that we only have a limited amount of time to live. **However, this book, which is also a 30-day devotional, is designed to inspire us to positively influence**

1

the world around us in the time God grants us. As we fulfill God's purposes for our lives, we should do what we can to make a tangible difference in the world. **Ultimately, God wants us to point people to Jesus Christ. But, in addition to getting others to know and believe in Jesus, we should do all we can to make the lives of the people around us better.**

In a story adapted from *The Star Thrower*, written by Loren Eiseley, a man was walking along the beach when he noticed a boy picking up something and throwing it into the water. When he asked the boy what he was doing, the boy said he was throwing starfish back into the ocean to keep them from dying. The man told the boy, "Don't you know there are many miles of beach with hundreds of stranded starfish? You can't possibly make a difference." After the man finished speaking, the boy reached down, picked up another starfish, threw it into the water, and said, "I made a difference for that one!"

We can learn a few lessons from this story. First, the boy decided to do whatever he could to make a difference. If we make a decision to do something, no matter how small, our action could make a significant impression on somebody's life.

Second, we might not be able to help e*very-one*, **but we can help** *someone.* The boy may not have saved every starfish on the beach, but he saved some of them.

Finally, no matter whether we are young or old, male or female, rich or not-so rich, famous or unknown, each one of us has the ability to perform some action that will make a difference in the lives of others.

The devotions in this book are divided into three categories: love, light, and legacy. The devotions on love discuss how we can make a difference by the way we show love to other people. The devotions on light focus on how we can make a difference by brightening up the world through our service, witness, and the way we live. The devotions on legacy concentrate on leaving something of value to our family, friends, and the world that will make a difference after we are gone.

Each devotion includes the following:

- A Scripture passage to read.
- One or more focus verses from the referenced passage.
- An exploration of the topic for the day.
- A one-statement summary of that day's main thought.
- Journal prompt questions and statements. If you take the time to meditate on and respond to these prompts, you will glean much more from the devotion.

Before you read each devotion, pray that God will open your eyes, mind, and heart to what He wants you to receive from that day's reading. Then at the end of the devotion, pray again that God will show you how to apply what you read to your life. **My prayer is that this book will inspire all of us to be people of God who are totally and completely committed to make a difference in the world while we have time.**

"Love" Devotions

The devotions in this section talk about ways we can make a difference by showing love to others.

"And he has given us this command: Anyone who loves God must also love their brother and sister."

— I John 4:21

DAY 1
MOTIVATED BY LOVE

Read 1 John 3:11–18.

"Dear children, let us not love with words or speech but with actions and in truth."
– 1 John 3:18

*M*aking a difference requires action, and one of the best motivators for action is love. The dictionary defines *love* as "a feeling of deep affection." However, *biblical love* is not based on feelings; rather, it is "a conscious decision to make someone else's best interest and well-being our priority."

Our focus verse says love should be demonstrated by actions, not just words. We can say that we want the world to be better. **However, if we want to make sure that some improvement takes place, we must do something, and love should be the driving force behind our actions.**

The greatest example of love moving someone to act is God's sending Jesus Christ to pay the penalty for our sins. John 3:16 tells us, *"For God so loved the world that he gave his one and only Son, that whoever believes in him shall not perish but have eternal life."* God's great love for us caused Him to give His Son so all mankind can have everlasting life. **Just as God's love for man drove Him to take action to benefit us, our love for others should compel us to do something to enhance people's lives.**

We should have a sacrificial and selfless love that causes us to work for the good of others.

Philippians 2:3 tells us, *"Do nothing out of selfish ambition or vain conceit. Rather, in humility value others above yourselves."* **When we value others and prioritize them over ourselves, we will make the sacrifices necessary to assist and serve them in whatever way we can.**

With strangers, showing love through our actions could mean going out of our way to aid someone who is in need. With friends and family, showing love through our actions could mean not being so focused on what we want to do for ourselves, but instead to sacrifice to spend time with our loved ones.

In every situation—whether we are dealing with family, friends, or strangers—our love for others should motivate us to take actions that will improve their situations, uplift their spirits, and, in general, make the world around us better.

If you want to make a difference
in the world, put your love
for others into action!

DAY 1
REFLECTION TIME

Do your family and friends know you love them?
If so, how? If not, what will you do to show
them?

_____

_____

_____

_____

_____

_____

_____

_____

_____

_____

What will you do today to demonstrate God's
love to someone in your community or city?

_____

_____

_____

_____

_____

_____

_____

_____

_____

_____

Day 2
Give Them Jesus

Read 1 John 4:7–12.

"This is how God showed his love among us: He sent his one and only Son into the world that we might live through him."
– 1 John 4:9

*I*n 1944 Hallmark Cards, Inc. adopted its famous slogan, "When you care enough to send the very best." A marketing and sales executive named C. E. Goodman created the slogan to encourage people to send Hallmark greeting cards to family and friends to express in words how much they care.

Long before Hallmark originated their slogan, God demonstrated how much He cared for us by sending His very best—His Son, Jesus Christ. Today's focus verse tells us God showed His love for us by sending Christ to give us eternal life. **Like God, we can show our love for others by giving them Jesus.**

When you love someone and want the very best for that person, what could be better than Jesus? **In fact, the most loving action we can take toward others is to tell them about the salvation that is available through Jesus Christ.** We need to do our best to address people's physical needs and assist them with the problems they encounter in their lives. But we should also be concerned about their souls and where they will spend eternity. In Mark 8:36, Jesus asked, *"What good is it for someone to gain the whole world, yet forfeit their soul?"* In other words, getting all the material goods a person wants does not benefit him if he does not have eternal life.

I recently saw a friend I had not seen in several years. At the end of our visit, we shared a warm embrace, and I told him I loved him. After he left, I was convicted by the Holy Spirit, and I asked myself, "How could I tell my friend I loved him and not talk to him about Christ?" He knew I believed in Jesus, and I had testified to him on many occasions about God's goodness in my life. However, I had never directly asked him where he stood with Christ. The next day, I called him and talked to him about Jesus. I was relieved and happy to hear him say he believed in Jesus.

If we truly love our family members and friends, we should talk to them about Jesus. As motivation to have these discussions, we can ask ourselves, "How can I say I love _____ [name of the family member or friend] and not talk to them about Jesus?" **If you love your family and friends enough to give them the very best, make sure you give them Jesus.***

If you want to make a difference in the world, tell your family and friends about the new life that is available in Jesus Christ!

---

* For assistance in telling others how they can believe in Jesus Christ for salvation, see the section titled "Witnessing About Christ" at the end of this book.

Day 2
Reflection Time

If you have not talked with your unsaved family members and friends about Jesus Christ, what's keeping you from doing so?

_____

_____

_____

_____

_____

_____

_____

_____

_____

What steps will you take to remove the barriers you listed? Make a commitment to talk about Jesus with those you know are unsaved by the end of this 30-day devotional.

_____

_____

_____

_____

_____

_____

_____

_____

_____

_____

Day 3
Let It Go

Read Ephesians 4:25–32.

"Be kind and compassionate to one another, forgiving each other, just as in Christ God forgave you."
– Ephesians 4:32

Some people just can't "let it go." They hold on to their anger against someone who may have wronged them days, weeks, months, and sometimes years earlier. Unforgiveness doesn't simply damage relationships; it destroys them. **Forgiveness involves letting go of ill feelings toward others and treating those individuals as if the offense never happened.** I want to examine three aspects of forgiveness that prayerfully will enable us to be more forgiving.

First, forgiveness shows compassion. The verse for today says being compassionate and loving toward people should move us to forgive them. **Just as God's love for us caused Him to forgive us through Jesus Christ, our love for others should cause us to forgive them when they offend us.**

Second, forgiveness is commanded by God. Forgiveness is not like an optional, elective course that students can take if they so choose. On the contrary, the fact that God commands us to forgive means forgiveness is mandatory and expected. Some people say they want to forgive that brother, sister, or friend, but they just cannot do it. In a sense, they are right. We cannot forgive on our own. **However, God would never command us to**

do something that He will not also enable us to do through the power of the Holy Spirit. If we really want to forgive others, God will help us to do so—even if we don't feel like it, or we think we are incapable of forgiving.

Third, forgiveness is a choice. Even though God empowers us to be forgiving, He will not force us to forgive. One reason people are unforgiving is they simply don't want to forgive; they choose to cling to the hurt someone caused them. In Matthew 6:14–15, Jesus said, *"For if you forgive other people when they sin against you, your heavenly Father will also forgive you. But if you do not forgive others their sins, your Father will not forgive your sins."* **Knowing that we need God to forgive us should motivate us to choose to forgive others.**

With each passing day, we have less time to spend with family and friends. If you need to reconcile with someone, don't delay a minute longer. Ask God to strengthen you to reach out to that person as soon as possible and make amends. Both of you will feel so much better!

If you want to make a difference
in the world, forgive others
when they offend you!

Day 3
Reflection Time

Would you (or do you) find it difficult to forgive someone who mistreats you? Why or why not?

_____

_____

_____

_____

_____

_____

_____

_____

_____

_____

Write a prayer asking God to give you the strength to forgive anyone who has wronged you in the past or who wrongs you in the future.

_____

_____

_____

_____

_____

_____

_____

_____

_____

_____

_____

DAY 4
CLOTHED WITH KINDNESS

Read Colossians 3:12–17.

"Therefore, as God's chosen people, holy and dearly loved, clothe yourselves with compassion, kindness, humility, gentleness and patience."
– Colossians 3:12

Kindness is "the quality of being friendly, generous, and considerate of others." Every day we live, we should try to make the world a better place in some fashion. One way we can do that is to show as much kindness as we can.

From today's focus verse, we see that as "God's chosen people," our lives should be characterized by kindness. God says we should be "clothed" with kindness. **The analogy of Christians wearing kindness like an article of clothing teaches us a couple of lessons.**

First, we should be kind at all times. When we get dressed, our clothes are on us no matter where we are. In the same manner, we should show kindness everywhere we go. **Just as you wouldn't leave your house without clothes, don't go anywhere without having a heart of kindness.**

Second, our kindness should not be affected or determined by how people act. We should be kind to others regardless of how they treat us. When you put on your clothes, they don't change based on who you are around. If you put on a red shirt, that shirt stays red no matter where you go. **Likewise, we should be kind to others in every situation, despite what they do or say or how they behave**

toward us.

In 1982 Anne Herbert drew attention to the importance of being kind when she coined the phrase "random acts of kindness." A *random act of kindness* is "an unplanned action that a person does in the course of a day that is designed to uplift someone in some way."

In addition to doing random acts of kindness, believers should also do *intentional acts of kindness*, which are "deliberate, planned actions that are meant to demonstrate the love of God to others." With intentional acts of kindness, we think about what we can do to brighten a person's day, bring a smile to his or her face, or let the person know he or she is on our mind. The good news is we don't have to choose between doing either random *or* intentional acts of kindness; we should do *both*! **The more kindness we show to others, the more love we spread throughout the world.**

If you want to make a difference
in the world, seek to be kind
to someone every day!

DAY 4
REFLECTION TIME

What intentional acts of kindness can you do today?

_____

_____

_____

_____

_____

_____

_____

_____

_____

_____

What can you do to remind yourself to show kindness to people on a regular basis?

_____

_____

_____

_____

_____

_____

_____

_____

_____

_____

_____

DAY 5
HONOR YOUR PARENTS

Read Ephesians 6:1–3.

"Honor your father and mother ..."
– Ephesians 6:2

*W*e are indebted to our father and mother because God brought us into the world through them. That fact alone should be reason enough for us to obey God's command to honor our parents.

The Greek word translated as *honor* in Ephesians 6:2 means "to revere, prize, and value." **To honor our parents means to respect them and treat them as valuable, priceless, and precious.** Based on these definitions for *honor*, today's focus verse tells us to "revere, prize, value, and respect our parents; treat them as precious and priceless."

To honor our parents requires more than just talk. **As used in this verse, "honor" is a verb, which means it requires action. In other words, we have to do something.** Some ways we can honor our parents include visiting them, respecting them in word (how we talk to them) and action (how we treat them), making them feel valued, and caring for them as they get older and need more assistance.

Maybe you feel like you have a valid reason for not honoring your parents. Perhaps they were not there for you when you needed them or they mistreated you in some way. **God's command to honor our parents is unconditional. Regardless of what may or may not have happened between our parents and us, God still commands us to**

honor them. God's command to honor our parents overrides and supersedes our thoughts and feelings.

If you are estranged from your parents, do what you can to reconcile with them while they and you are still alive. **If you are harboring a grudge against your parents, ask God to give you the ability to forgive them, so you can honor them.** (For more on forgiveness, see the Day 3 devotion titled, "Let It Go.")

Unfortunately, some people don't have their parents with them any longer. If that is your situation, maybe you can honor someone who was or is like a parent to you. If your parents are still living, don't take them for granted. Thank God for them and enjoy the time God gives you with them.

While our focus verse specifically mentions "father and mother," we should also honor our grandparents, aunts, uncles, and any other older relatives in our family while we can.

Don't wait; honor your parents (or older relatives) today, while you are still able to do so.

If you want to make a difference in the world, show honor and respect to your parents, grand- parents, and other older family members!

DAY 5
REFLECTION TIME

What will you do to show honor and respect to your parents or other older family members?

_____

_____

_____

_____

_____

_____

_____

_____

_____

_____

Which older members of your church or community can you honor?

_____

_____

_____

_____

_____

_____

_____

_____

_____

_____

DAY 6
GIVE THEM THEIR FLOWERS

Read 1 Thessalonians 1:1–10.

"We always thank God for all of you and continually mention you in our prayers."
– 1 Thessalonians 1:2

*I*t's easy to take people for granted, especially the ones we see on a regular basis. **The saying "give people their flowers while they can smell them" means we should tell others how much they mean to us and show our appreciation while they are still alive.**

We should be thankful to God for the people He puts in our lives and let them know we are grateful to and for them. In today's reading, Paul told the Thessalonian believers that he, Silas, and Timothy thanked God for them.

Do you need to show appreciation to someone for something they did for you? Has someone gone out of his or her way to assist you, given you money when you needed it, or helped you out of a tight jam? Did someone give you encouragement when you were down, offer godly counsel when you didn't know what to do, stay by you during tough times, or support you as a friend?

You probably thanked these people then, but maybe you never told them how significant their presence and actions were in your life. Now is the time to tell them you are thankful to God for them. **When people do something for us that they don't have to do, it makes sense to thank them.**

The following are three benefits to acknowledging someone for something they did. **First, acknowledging others' kindness will make them feel good that their generosity was recognized and appreciated.**

Second, acknowledging others' helpfulness will encourage them to continue aiding people. Knowing that their gracious acts were appreciated will fuel their desire to keep doing what they can to bless others.

Third, recognizing that others helped us will inspire us to follow their example and do a kind deed for someone else. We will reflect on the fact that someone went above and beyond the call of duty to assist us, and we will be motivated to do the same for others.

No one has to do anything for us. When they do, let us use our words and actions to show appreciation to them.

If you want to make a difference in the world, show appreciation to the people God puts in your life!

DAY 6
REFLECTION TIME

Who do you need to thank God for and express appreciation to?

_____

_____

_____

_____

_____

_____

_____

_____

_____

_____

What will you do to make sure they know how grateful you are to them for all they did for you?

_____

_____

_____

_____

_____

_____

_____

_____

_____

_____

_____

Day 7
Encouragement Matters

Read Acts 20:1–6.

"He traveled through that area, speaking many words of encouragement to the people, and finally arrived in Greece."

– Acts 20:2

*D*iscouragement may afflict a person for a variety of reasons, including health concerns because of sickness in their body, relationship concerns because of family issues, safety concerns because of violence in their community, and financial concerns because of the state of the economy. In some cases, people can become discouraged when their lives aren't going the way they desire.

While we might not be able to fix many of these causes of discouragement, we can encourage those who are disheartened. To *encourage* **means "to give support, confidence, hope, or courage to someone."** In today's reading, the apostle Paul spoke "many words of encouragement to the people." **As we go through the day, we should keep our eyes and ears open for opportunities to encourage someone.** Encouraging others is free and doesn't have to take an abundance of time.

As we see from Paul's example, our words can be a great source of encouragement to others. Ephesians 4:29 tells us, *"Do not let any unwholesome talk come out of your mouths, but only what is helpful for building others up according to their needs, that it may benefit those who listen."*

Encouraging others results in several positive

outcomes. **First, our encouragement can give someone the confidence to continue on instead of giving up.** In my first semester of college, my grades were very low. I was discouraged and ready to drop out. However, my dad encouraged me to keep trying and said he believed I could do better. I heeded his advice, improved my grades, and, thank God, I ultimately graduated. The encouragement I received from my dad played a major role in my staying in school and getting my degree.

Second, offering encouragement can give hope to someone who feels hopeless. We never know how an encouraging word can cause someone to look at their situation from a different, more positive perspective. If someone is feeling depressed, a word of encouragement can lift their spirits. Proverbs 12:25 states, *"Anxiety weighs down the heart, but a kind word cheers it up."*

Third, encouraging others lets them know we care about them. Sometimes, we are discouraged when we go through difficult times, and we feel like we are all by ourselves. Having someone encourage and uplift us tells us we are not as alone as we think we are. Of course, we know God is always with us, but having that human person walking alongside and encouraging us is very beneficial. **Let us be intentional and make an effort to encourage someone today.**

If you want to make a difference in the world, encourage others on a regular basis!

DAY 7
REFLECTION TIME

Who do you know who needs encouragement? How will you encourage them?

_____

_____

_____

_____

_____

_____

_____

_____

_____

_____

Write a prayer asking God to enable you to recognize and take advantage of opportunities to encourage others.

_____

_____

_____

_____

_____

_____

_____

_____

_____

_____

Day 8
Love Is Patient

Read 1 Corinthians 13:4–7.

"Love is patient, love is kind. It does not envy, it does not boast, it is not proud."
– 1 Corinthians 13:4

*Y*ou have probably heard the adage, "Patience is a virtue." I believe patience is more than a commendable quality. **Patience is a way to show people we love them.** *Patience* can be defined as "the ability to accept or tolerate trouble, inconvenience, suffering, and difficult circumstances and people without getting angry, annoyed, or upset."

The focus verse says, "Love is patient." People will not always act the way we want them to, but if we love them, we will be patient and understanding with them. Patience enables us to show love and make a difference in the world in several ways.

First, patience allows us to live more at peace with others by minimizing conflicts and arguments. Proverbs 15:18 declares, *"A hot-tempered person stirs up conflict, but the one who is patient calms a quarrel."* An argument takes two people. If one person is emotional and angry but the other person remains patient and calm, an argument will be prevented.

Second, patience helps us to be less judgmental of people because of what they say or do. Matthew 7:3 states, *"Why do you look at the speck of sawdust in your brother's eye and pay no attention to the plank in your own eye?"* Recognizing that we are not perfect and have our own problems will give us the patience to accept others as they are and to be more tolerant of them.

Third, patience empowers us to represent Jesus Christ well. We shine a negative light on Christ when we get impatient, annoyed, and angry at the inconveniences caused by others. Being patient in these situations allows us to be better witnesses for Jesus. James 1:20 tells us, *"Because human anger does not produce the righteousness that God desires."*

As we pursue patience, we must understand that we cannot be patient in our own strength. Galatians 5:22–23 (NLT) say, *"But the Holy Spirit produces this kind of fruit in our lives: love, joy, peace, patience, kindness, goodness, faithfulness, gentleness, and self-control. There is no law against these things!"* **We must be submissive to the Holy Spirit and allow Him to produce the fruit of patience in our lives.**

We cannot correct everything that is wrong in society, but being patient results in a beautiful chain reaction that can improve the state of the world. The more people are patient with each other, the less violence there will be. The less violence there is, the more peace there will be. The more peace there is, the better the world will be. **We can do our part to make the world a better place when we show love for others by being patient with them.**

If you want to make a difference in the world, be patient with others!

DAY 8
REFLECTION TIME

What do people do that causes you to become impatient, annoyed, or upset?

_____

_____

_____

_____

_____

_____

_____

_____

_____

_____

What will you do to be more patient with people in the future?

_____

_____

_____

_____

_____

_____

_____

_____

_____

_____

_____

_____

DAY 9
THE POWER OF PRAYER

Read James 5:13–18.

"... The prayer of a righteous person is powerful and effective."

– James 5:16

"*I* wish I could do more for you, but all I can do is pray." Maybe someone has made that statement to you when you were going through a difficult time. Or perhaps you said these words to a friend who was having trouble.

Wanting to do as much as we can to aid someone is admirable. As we pray for others, God may use us to be the answer to our own prayers by leading us to take action to assist the ones who are in need. However, when we cannot help in a tangible way, saying, "*All* I can do is pray" minimizes the importance and power of prayer. It's like saying prayer is simply a token act that we do as a last resort. **On the contrary, praying for someone is one of the best and most loving actions we can take for them.**

Today's focus verse says prayer is "powerful and effective" when offered by a person who has been made righteous through faith in Jesus Christ. **Since prayer is powerful and effective, the more we pray for the people around us, the greater impact we can have on the world.**

Job 1:5 tells us that Job regularly sacrificed burnt offerings for his children, in case they had sinned against God. In like fashion, we should pray for God's grace and mercy for our family and friends on a regular basis. **If we know of anyone who is not a Christian, we should specifically pray that God would soften their heart and that they would believe in Jesus.**

Too often, we wait until there is trouble or a problem before we pray. However, in Luke 18:1, Jesus tells us we should *"always pray and not give up."* Jesus did more than tell us to pray; He prayed Himself. Luke 5:16 states, *"But Jesus often withdrew to lonely places and prayed."* **Like Jesus, we should have a lifestyle of prayer. Prayer should be SOP—standard operating procedure—for our lives.**

We should pray for everyone, but we should especially pray for family and friends because we have more intimate knowledge about their specific situations and needs. Praying for those close to us is powerful, but letting them hear specifically what we are praying for them will be even more impactful. They will feel the love and sincerity in our voice as they hear what we are asking God to do for them. They will know that we are concerned enough to pray for them. **Let us endeavor to positively affect the world by praying regularly for others.**

If you want to make a difference in the world, pray for others!

DAY 9
REFLECTION TIME

Do you think God is satisfied with your prayer life? If so, why? If not, what do you need to change?

_____

_____

_____

_____

_____

_____

_____

_____

_____

Make a list of the people you will pray for and what their needs are. Commit to pray for them regularly.

_____

_____

_____

_____

_____

_____

_____

_____

_____

_____

_____

DAY 10
IT'S ALL IN A TOUCH

Read Luke 15:11–24.

"So he got up and went to his father. But while he was still a long way off, his father saw him and was filled with compassion for him; he ran to his son, threw his arms around him and kissed him."
– Luke 15:20

*T*oday's reading has been called "The Parable of the Lost Son" and "The Story of the Prodigal Son." However, this passage of Scripture could also be given another title: "The Story of the Loving Father." In the parable, the son demanded that his father give him his portion of the father's estate immediately instead of waiting until the father passed away. The father obliged the son and gave him his inheritance. The son took the money and wasted it on reckless living. Eventually, the son came to his senses and returned home.

Our focus verse says when the father saw his son, he was "filled with compassion for him." **The father showed the son that he still loved him through physical touch: he "threw his arms around him and kissed him."**

In his book titled, *The 5 Love Languages*, author Gary Chapman lists physical touch as one of the five ways spouses can show love to one another. Using physical touch to communicate affection is not limited to marriage and romantic relationships, but can also be applied to platonic and family relationships. **We can quickly and easily express our love for family members and friends through a**

hug, a kiss on the cheek, a pat on the back, or a stroke on the arm. I am sure the son in the parable felt the authenticity of the father's love for him as a result of the father's hug and kiss.

Today, the pace of life is seemingly so fast, and we are so busy that we don't take the time to touch. In our technology-driven society, seeing couples walking down the street totally engrossed in their mobile devices instead of holding hands or hugging is a common occurrence.

Physical touch is beneficial because it lets others know we care and we are there for them, gives comfort and reassurance to someone who may be feeling down, strengthens the emotional bond we have with our loved ones, and increases the closeness we feel with our family members and friends.

Physical touch is appropriate for all ages. Parents can hug their children, regardless of their age. Siblings of any age can hug one another. Younger family members can show their love for older family members by embracing them. My great-nephew, Carter, who is eight years old at the time of this writing, hugs me every time he sees me. Those hugs let me know he loves me.

Let us make it a priority to show our love for others through physical touch while we still can and while our loved ones can still feel the depth of our affection.

If you want to make a difference in the world, express your love for others through physical touch!

DAY 10
REFLECTION TIME

When has a hug, a kiss, or a touch from a family member or friend made you feel loved?

_____

_____

_____

_____

_____

_____

_____

_____

_____

_____

_____

Who do you need to express your love for through physical touch? When will you do it?

_____

_____

_____

_____

_____

_____

_____

_____

_____

_____

_____

_____

"Light" Devotions

The devotions in this section talk about ways we can make a difference by letting our light shine to brighten up the world.

"In the same way, let your light shine before others, that they may see your good deeds and glorify your Father in heaven."
— Matthew 5:16

DAY 11
LET YOUR LIGHT SHINE
(PART 1)

Read Matthew 5:14–16.

"In the same way, let your light shine before others, that they may see your good deeds and glorify your Father in heaven."
– Matthew 5:16

*H*ave you ever thought about how challenging our lives would be if there were no light in the world? Without some type of natural or even artificial light, doing anything would be difficult, if not impossible. The fact that creating light (Genesis 1:3) was the first action God took after He made the heavens and the earth shows us exactly how important and essential light is.

Light overcomes literal darkness, which allows us to function effectively and efficiently. However, in addition to literal darkness, there is also figurative darkness in the world due to the sinfulness and selfishness of mankind. This figurative darkness causes people to lie, steal, cheat, deceive, and perform all kinds of hurtful acts against others.

In Matthew 5:14, Jesus said His followers are the light of the world. **We shine our light when the actions we take, the deeds we do, and the words we say counteract the figurative darkness around us, making the world a better place.**

We can ascertain several thoughts about being the light of the world from today's reading. **First, verse 15 tells us we should not hide our light, but we should let people see it ("put it on its stand").**

If you turn on the light in a closet and close the door, the light doesn't help anyone outside the closet. We hide our light when we keep to ourselves and don't assist people when we have the ability to help them. **On the other hand, the more we get involved in the community and with other people, the more our light can shine and the more we can be a blessing to others.**

Second, we cannot light up the whole world, but we can shine light on the part of the world where we are. Verse 15 tells us that if we don't conceal our light, what we do can illuminate "everyone in the house," i.e., the people around us. **We might not be able to help everybody, but if we look hard enough, we will find someone whose life we can brighten by shining our light.**

Third, verse 16 tells us one way we can shine our light is by doing good deeds. A *good deed* is "anything we do that lifts someone up, lightens their burdens, or gives them relief or assistance in some way." James 2:26 tells us, *"As the body without the spirit is dead, so faith without deeds is dead."* Our good deeds give evidence that our faith in Jesus Christ is genuine. **Doing good for others should be the rule in our lives, not the exception.**

Tomorrow's devotion will further address what it means to let our light shine. **In the meantime, I encourage you to be intentional about being a light in your world today.**

If you want to make a difference
in the world, let your light
shine by doing good deeds!

DAY 11
REFLECTION TIME

In what ways can you make your neighborhood or community a better place?

_____

_____

_____

_____

_____

_____

_____

_____

_____

_____

What good deeds do you perform on a regular basis that indicate your light is shining?

_____

_____

_____

_____

_____

_____

_____

_____

_____

_____

_____

Day 12
Let Your Light Shine
(Part 2)

Read Matthew 5:14–16.

"In the same way, let your light shine before others, that they may see your good deeds and glorify your Father in heaven."

– Matthew 5:16

*Y*esterday's devotion explored three aspects of being the light of the world. Today, we will look at three more truths related to being a light.

Fourth, the word "let" in today's verse tells us that whether or not our light shines is up to us. We can consciously and intentionally shine our light by submitting ourselves to the Holy Spirit, obeying God's commands, and allowing Christ to live, speak, and serve through us. When we do these things, we can make a difference in the world.

Fifth, even though our focus verse says "your light," we must realize that the only light we have comes from God as He lives in and through us. Scientists inform us that the moon does not make its own light, and that moonlight is actually sunlight that reflects off the moon. Just as the moon reflects the *sun*, we as children of God should reflect the *Son*, Jesus Christ, through the way we live, behave, and treat others.

Every believer has a light they can shine, but everybody's light may not be the same and may not shine the same way. God gave us our own individual spiritual gifts, abilities, and personalities that allow us to shine in the world in our own unique way. The way one person shines and affects the world may be completely different from another person. **What matters is not *how* we make a difference in the world, but *that* we make an impact in some way.** We should let our light shine in the way God designed and intended it to shine.

Sixth, when we let our light shine through our good deeds, we should not take any credit for what we do. On the contrary, we should make sure that we point people to God so He gets the praise. Verse 16 lets us know that the good deeds we do should cause people to glorify God. Whatever good deeds we do are only possible because God gives us the strength and ability to do them. In John 15:5, Jesus said, *"... Apart from me you can do nothing."* **Since we cannot do anything without the Lord, it stands to reason that He should be recognized and acknowledged for everything we do.**

You have a light, and God wants you to shine your light in such a way that others are blessed and He is praised. Won't you let your light shine today so you can make a difference in the world while you can?

If you want to make a difference
in the world, be intentional
about letting your light shine!

DAY 12
REFLECTION TIME

What evidence do you see in your life that indicates your light is shining?

_____

_____

_____

_____

_____

_____

_____

_____

_____

_____

_____

Write a prayer asking God to show you where and how He wants you to shine your light so you can brighten your part of the world.

_____

_____

_____

_____

_____

_____

_____

_____

_____

_____

_____

DAY 13
LIVE AS CHILDREN OF LIGHT

Read Ephesians 5:1–13.

"For you were once darkness, but now you are light in the Lord. Live as children of light."
– Ephesians 5:8

"**B**efore" and "after" pictures are used to show that something has changed. In most cases, these pictures not only illustrate that a change has taken place, but they also draw attention to the extent or magnitude of that change.

In our focus verse, the apostle Paul gives a "before" and "after" picture of believers. He says we "were once darkness" (i.e., *before* we became Christians), but now we "are light in the Lord" (i.e., *after* we believed in Jesus Christ). **The contrast between the way we used to be and the way we are now should be evident in how we live and as obvious as the difference between light and darkness.** We are to live as "children of light."

As children of light, the difference between how we were "before" and how we are "after" should be seen in several areas. **First, our character should be different than it was before.** We should live righteous lives that reflect the teachings of God's Word. Verse 9 of today's reading says, *"For the fruit of the light consists in all goodness, righteousness and truth."* Also, Titus 2:12 declares, *"It* [God's grace] *teaches us to say 'No' to ungodliness and worldly passions, and to live self-controlled, upright and godly lives in this present age."* **When we live a godly, righteous life on a** consistent basis, we shed light on the parts of the world we touch.

Second, as children of light, the way we talk should be different than it was before. Proverbs 12:18 says, *"The words of the reckless pierce like swords, but the tongue of the wise brings healing."* In addition, Proverbs 16:24 states, *"Gracious words are a honeycomb, sweet to the soul and healing to the bones."* These verses let us know that when we make negative, hurtful, and unkind comments to others, we tear them down. **On the other hand, we brighten others' lives when we say what enhances them and builds them up.**

Third, as children of light, the way we interact with people should be different than it was before. Ephesians 4:2 tells us, *"Be completely humble and gentle; be patient, bearing with one another in love."* Thinking about how gentle, patient, and loving God has been to us should move us to treat people in the same manner. **We allow the light of God's love to shine through us when we are nice, calm, and understanding with people who are rude and disrespectful to us.**

Thankfully, God has given us all we need to live as children of light. Second Peter 1:3 tells us, *"His divine power has given us everything we need for a godly life through our knowledge of him who called us by his own glory and goodness."* **Won't you commit yourself to live as a child of light?**

If you want to make a difference in the world, live as a child of light everywhere you go!

DAY 13
REFLECTION TIME

In your own words, state what it means to you to live as a "child of light."

_____

_____

_____

_____

_____

_____

_____

_____

_____

_____

In what areas do you need to change your "after" picture so your life lines up more with God's Word?

_____

_____

_____

_____

_____

_____

_____

_____

_____

_____

DAY 14
VOLUNTEERS NEEDED

Read Galatians 6:1–10.

"Therefore, as we have opportunity, let us do good to all people, especially to those who belong to the family of believers."

– Galatians 6:10

*E*ighty-six thousand, four hundred. That is how many seconds God gives us in each twenty-four-hour day. God graciously allows us to decide how we want to use this time. **If we want to be lights and brighten our corner of the world, we should use some of this time volunteering to aid others.**

This devotion centers on predetermined or planned service, such as when we volunteer individually or with a group or organization. From today's reading, we can learn several principles with regard to using our time to serve others.

First, we should always have a desire to help people. Verse 9 says, *"Let us not become weary in doing good, for at the proper time we will reap a harvest if we do not give up."* Sometimes in the workplace, we might reach a point where we are no longer enthusiastic about doing that job. The tasks become boring or monotonous, and we want to do something different. Such should not be the case regarding doing good for people. Too many people need assistance for us to get tired of serving them. **Recognizing how much God has blessed us should spark us to use our time to be a blessing to others through our service.**

Second, we should take advantage of every opportunity we get to aid people. Our focus verse (v. 10) says we should help others "as we have opportunity." When we look around, we can easily see opportunities to assist people. Many worthy organizations meet the needs of people who are less fortunate. We can influence our communities for the better by serving with these organizations.

The opportunities to help are readily available. The real issue is whether we will make it a priority to take advantage of those opportunities. Instead of saying we don't have time to volunteer, we should rearrange our priorities so we have time to serve others and make a difference in their lives. Galatians 5:13 states, *"You, my brothers and sisters, were called to be free. But do not use your freedom to indulge the flesh; rather, serve one another humbly in love."* Will you use your freedom to serve others?

Third, we should not put restrictions on who we help. We should "do good to all people" (v. 10). Romans 2:11 declares, *"For God does not show favoritism."* Likewise, when it comes to helping others, we should not show partiality. **We should try to benefit as many people as we can without bias or discrimination.**

One of the best uses of the health, strength, and time God gives us is to aid others. Our service to others makes their lives better and may shine a much-needed ray of hope on their situations.

If you want to make a difference in
the world, volunteer your time
to bless and serve others!

DAY 14
REFLECTION TIME

What organizations or groups can you volunteer with in your community?

_____

_____

_____

_____

_____

_____

_____

_____

_____

_____

How will you rearrange or modify your schedule so you can have more time to volunteer?

_____

_____

_____

_____

_____

_____

_____

_____

_____

_____

_____

DAY 15
BE A GOOD NEIGHBOR

Read Luke 10:25–37.

"'Which of these three do you think was a neighbor to the man who fell into the hands of robbers?' The expert in the law replied, 'The one who had mercy on him.' Jesus told him, 'Go and do likewise.'"
– Luke 10:36–37

The previous devotion dealt with giving our time to participate in predetermined or planned volunteer service. **This devotion encourages us to be a light by helping others spontaneously as we go through our day.**

In today's reading, a man (assumed to be a Jew) was attacked by robbers. His attackers took his clothes, beat him, and left him severely injured. Upon seeing the badly beaten man, both a priest and a Levite passed by the man without rendering aid. However, when a Samaritan man saw him, he bandaged his wounds, took him to an inn, and cared for him.

Yesterday's devotion mentioned three principles for helping people: 1) have a desire to help, 2) take advantage of every opportunity to aid others, and 3) don't put restrictions on who we help. Notice how the Samaritan applied all three of these principles to spontaneously assist the man in need.

First, the Samaritan desired to help the man who had been robbed and beaten. We know this because he did not avoid the man, like the priest and Levite did. **We never know when we will encounter someone who needs assistance; there-**

fore, we should always be willing to aid people in need. We can cultivate a desire to help others by asking God to give us a servant's heart.

Second, the Samaritan took advantage of the opportunity to aid the injured man. Though not pre-planned, when the Samaritan saw someone with a need, he made the decision to meet that need. **When God gives us an opportunity to assist someone, we should step up and do what we can.** We should always be prepared to do what is right according to the Word of God.

Third, even though the beaten man was of a different nationality, the Samaritan did not discriminate against him; he took care of him anyway. **Who the person in need is should not determine whether or not we assist them. If we are able to benefit someone, we should.**

When Jesus asked the expert in the law who was a neighbor to the man who was robbed, he said, "The one who had mercy on him." Jesus told him (and He is telling us), "Go and do likewise." **That is, we should have mercy on others and do good to them.**

Let us be obedient to the prompting and guidance of the Holy Spirit and do what we can to assist those who are in need. In that way, we can be a light and make a difference in someone's life.

If you want to make a difference
in the world, be a good neighbor,
and help people in need!

DAY 15
REFLECTION TIME

What steps will you take to ensure you notice and take advantage of opportunities to help others?

_____

_____

_____

_____

_____

_____

_____

_____

_____

_____

_____

Write a prayer asking God to compel you to assist others whenever you can.

_____

_____

_____

_____

_____

_____

_____

_____

_____

_____

_____

DAY 16
THE BLESSING OF GIVING

Read Acts 20:32–35.

"In everything I did, I showed you that by this kind of hard work we must help the weak, remembering the words the Lord Jesus himself said: 'It is more blessed to give than to receive.'"
– Acts 20:35

*A*s far back as the time of Moses, God has commanded His people to take care of the poor. For example, Deuteronomy 15:7–8 say, *"If anyone is poor among your fellow Israelites in any of the towns of the land the LORD your God is giving you, do not be hardhearted or tightfisted toward them. Rather, be openhanded and freely lend them whatever they need."* Similarly, Acts 2:44–45 illustrate how believers in the early church gave to those in need: *"All the believers were together and had everything in common. They sold property and possessions to give to anyone who had need."* These verses teach that we are to give to those who do not have what they need.

Our focus verse for today says we must "help the weak." In this context, *weak* refers to "people who are poor or need assistance." Acts 20:35 concludes with the words of Jesus: *"It is more blessed to give than to receive."*

At first glance, the thought that it's better to give money away than to receive it might seem paradoxical. But when you think about it, the fact that we are in a position to give means God blessed us with enough to provide for ourselves and still have something left over to meet the needs of others. **If God blesses us financially, we should be willing to share what we have received with others.**

When my oldest son, Joey Jr., was ten years old, he and I were talking about giving to people in need. He told me that when we give to the needy, we make two people feel good. I asked him what he meant. **He said, "The people we give to feel good because they receive what they need, and we feel good because we are able to help somebody."** I thought this explanation was very profound for a ten-year old!

In addition to the needy person and the giver feeling good, the Scriptures tell us God is also pleased. Hebrews 13:16 states, *"And do not forget to do good and to share with others, for with such sacrifices God is pleased."* **When we use the material blessings God has given us to aid those who are less fortunate, God is pleased, and we shine light in the world by bringing hope to the people who need it.**

If you want to make a difference in the world, use your financial resources to help the less fortunate!

DAY 16
REFLECTION TIME

If God has blessed you to be able to give financially to people in need, do you do it? If so, why? If not, why not?

_____

_____

_____

_____

_____

_____

_____

_____

_____

_____

_____

What needs or causes are you so passionate about that you give financially to address them?

_____

_____

_____

_____

_____

_____

_____

_____

_____

_____

_____

DAY 17
THE LIGHT OF SALVATION
(PART 1)

Read Acts 13:44–48.

"For this is what the Lord has commanded us: 'I have made you a light for the Gentiles, that you may bring salvation to the ends of the earth.'"
– Acts 13:47

*I*n the Day 2 devotion titled "Give Them Jesus," I stated that we can show love to family and friends by telling them they can be saved by believing in Jesus Christ. **But our witness for Christ should not be limited only to the people we know. We should tell everyone about Jesus, whether or not we know them.**

In our focus verse, the Lord told Paul and Barnabas that He made them a "light for the Gentiles" that they might "bring salvation to the ends of the earth." **God has also made us lights so we can show Christ to the people we encounter in our daily activities.**

One way we can take the gospel to the "ends of the earth" is by being a foreign missionary. Many people give up their comfortable lifestyles to go to other countries as missionaries to tell people about Jesus. However, we don't have to travel overseas to witness for Christ. **Many people in our own neighborhoods, communities, and cities need to hear about Jesus' death and resurrection.** In Matthew 9:37, we read: *"Then he [Jesus] said to his disciples, 'The harvest is plentiful but the workers are few.'"* Jesus is sending us into the harvest of the world to tell people about Him.

Some Bible scholars estimate that the apostle Paul traveled approximately 10,000 miles on land and sea during his missionary journeys to spread the gospel of Jesus Christ; and he didn't have the luxury of an automobile or airplane! **If Paul could travel that many miles to tell people about Jesus, surely, we can go to our next-door neighbors, across the street, and throughout our neighborhoods to share the gospel.**

People everywhere need to hear the good news of Jesus Christ. Romans 10:14 asks, *"How, then, can they call on the one they have not believed in? And how can they believe in the one of whom they have not heard? And how can they hear without someone preaching to them?"* We are the "someone" God wants to use to spread the gospel to others! **Everywhere we go, we have an opportunity to tell people about Jesus.** Some places we can witness for Christ include our workplace, stores, restaurants, fitness centers, community gatherings, and festivals, to name a few.

Since the next moment is not promised to any of us, we should tell people about Jesus whenever and wherever we can. **What better way to bring light to the world than to tell others that God offers them eternal life through Jesus Christ?***

If you want to make a difference in the world, tell people about Jesus whenever and wherever you can!

---

* For assistance in telling others how they can believe in Jesus Christ for salvation, see the section titled "Witnessing About Christ" at the end of this book.

DAY 17
REFLECTION TIME

Make a list of places you go where you will witness for Jesus Christ.

_____

_____

_____

_____

_____

_____

_____

_____

_____

_____

_____

Write a prayer asking God to give you the words to say and the boldness to witness for Christ everywhere you go.

_____

_____

_____

_____

_____

_____

_____

_____

_____

_____

_____

DAY 18
THE LIGHT OF SALVATION
(PART 2)

Read Acts 13:44–48.

"For this is what the Lord has commanded us: 'I have made you a light for the Gentiles, that you may bring salvation to the ends of the earth.'"
– Acts 13:47

*T*he previous devotion addressed how we can be a light in the world by telling others they can have eternal life by believing in Jesus Christ's death and resurrection. This devotion will look at some key points to remember as we talk to others about Jesus.

First, our witness for Christ must be done with love. We should love others enough to want them to be saved. First Thessalonians 4:9 says, *"Now about your love for one another we do not need to write to you, for you yourselves have been taught by God to love each other."*

Second, our witness for Christ must be done with prayer. As it relates to witnessing, we should make four requests of the Lord every day: 1) send someone to us with whom we can share Christ, 2) touch their hearts to be receptive and respond positively to the gospel, 3) give us the words to say to them, and 4) give us the boldness to speak for Him. Ephesians 6:19–20 state, *"Pray also for me, that whenever I speak, words may be given me so that I will fearlessly make known the mystery of the gospel, for which I am an ambassador in chains. Pray that I may declare it fearlessly, as I should."*

Third, our witness for Christ must be done with power. If we want to be effective witnesses for Jesus, we need the power of the Holy Spirit. Acts 1:8 tells us, *"But you will receive power when the Holy Spirit comes on you; and you will be my witnesses in Jerusalem, and in all Judea and Samaria, and to the ends of the earth."*

Fourth, our witness for Christ must be done with urgency. We don't know when our last moment on earth will be, so we should make it a priority to talk to others about Christ before it's too late. John 9:4 declares, *"As long as it is day, we must do the works of him who sent me. Night is coming, when no one can work."*

Fifth, our witness for Christ must be done with regularity. Spreading the gospel of Christ to others should be something we do daily—not just at certain times of the year or as part of an organized evangelistic outreach activity. Jesus commanded us, *"Therefore go and make disciples of all nations, baptizing them in the name of the Father and of the Son and of the Holy Spirit, and teaching them to obey everything I have commanded you. And surely I am with you always, to the very end of the age"* (Matthew 28:19–20).

Let us be committed to make a difference in the world by shining the light of the gospel of Jesus Christ on others so they can be saved.*

> *If you want to make a difference in the world, lovingly tell people about Jesus with urgency and regularity!*

---

* For assistance in telling others how they can believe in Jesus Christ for salvation, see the section titled "Witnessing About Christ" at the end of this book.

DAY 18
REFLECTION TIME

What will you do to remind yourself of the urgency of witnessing about Christ to the people with whom you interact?

_____

_____

_____

_____

_____

_____

_____

_____

_____

_____

_____

Write a prayer asking God to send someone to you so you can witness to them about Christ.

_____

_____

_____

_____

_____

_____

_____

_____

_____

_____

_____

Day 19
Contagious Joy

Read Philippians 4:1–5.

"Rejoice in the Lord always. I will say it again: Rejoice!"
– Philippians 4:4

We live in a world where negative events in the local and national news, as well as in our individual lives, are all too common. Consequently, we find ourselves complaining about what is going on. However, complaining can become contagious and propagate an atmosphere of negativity.

Instead of complaining about what's happening, someone needs to be a light and brighten others' day. Let us choose to be people who uplifts others by spreading joy.

Joy can be defined as "extreme happiness or cheerfulness; gladness of heart; satisfaction and contentment." Earthly joy comes as a result of what happens to us. However, that kind of joy is temporary and usually goes away when whatever prompted the joy ends. **On the other hand, true joy, which comes from the Lord and is given to us by the Holy Spirit is lasting!** Galatians 5:22–23 (NLT) tell us, *"But the Holy Spirit produces this kind of fruit in our lives: love, joy, peace, patience, kindness, goodness, faithfulness, gentleness, and self-control. There is no law against these things!"* **Since the Holy Spirit gives us joy and He lives inside every believer, we all have the ability to be joyful.**

Our focus verse says we should rejoice in the

Lord at all times. **Rejoicing is the outward expression of the joy we have on the inside and is manifested in the way we live, what we say, and what we do.** Our joy should be evident by our smile, our upbeat spirit, our warm and gracious speech, and our positive attitude. Philippians 4:8 tells us, *"Finally, brothers and sisters, whatever is true, whatever is noble, whatever is right, whatever is pure, whatever is lovely, whatever is admirable—if anything is excellent or praiseworthy—think about such things."* **Positive thoughts lead to positive words and actions.** How does it look for someone to testify, "I am a joyful Christian," but that joy cannot be seen on the person's face or in their life?

You may be wondering how you can rejoice when you are going through times of difficulty. Because our joy originates in the Lord, it is not tied to external circumstances. Therefore, even in the midst of trouble, through the power of the Holy Spirit, a believer can exhibit joy. James 1:2–3 state, *"Consider it pure joy, my brothers and sisters, whenever you face trials of many kinds, because you know that the testing of your faith produces perseverance."*

Just as complaining and negativity can be contagious, so can joy. In good and bad times, God calls His children to exhibit joy. In doing so, we might inspire the people watching us to be joyful also. **Let us seek to spread joy everywhere we go so we can brighten up the world around us.**

If you want to make a difference in the world, exhibit the joy of the Lord everywhere you go!

61

DAY 19
REFLECTION TIME

What will you do to make sure your joy is evident to the people you interact with each day?

_____

_____

_____

_____

_____

_____

_____

_____

_____

_____

_____

Write a prayer asking God to enable you to be joyful despite your circumstances.

_____

_____

_____

_____

_____

_____

_____

_____

_____

_____

_____

DAY 20
WHAT'S FOR DINNER?

Read Matthew 25:34–40.

"For I was hungry and you gave me something to eat ..."

– Matthew 25:35

*H*unger is a global problem affecting many people around the world. The World Food Program (WFP), which operates in 78 countries, estimated that in 2023 over 333 million people didn't know where their next meal would come from. This hunger indicator is more than twice as high as it was in 2020.

In today's reading, Jesus said when we feed the hungry, it is like feeding Him. **One of the ways we can make the world a better place is by doing what we can to feed the people who don't have food to eat.**

One of the challenges that makes the hunger problem so difficult to tackle is that some people who are not directly touched by a food shortage may not be sensitive to the issue. **However, the fact that a person has all the food he needs should not keep him from recognizing the severity of the problem and doing something to benefit those who are affected.**

Many times, when the subject of hunger comes up, our minds immediately go to people in other countries. But we can find hungry people right in our own country, state, and city who we can supply with food. **Too many people in the world have been blessed financially for so many people to be**

without food.

As people of God, we should have a heart of empathy and be willing to do our part to meet the needs of those who are hungry whenever we can. First John 3:17 says, *"If anyone has material possessions and sees a brother or sister in need but has no pity on them, how can the love of God be in that person?"* **Using the material and financial resources God has given us to assist in feeding the people who don't have food shows the love of God and is one way we can shine light in the world.**

Like in the starfish story, we may not be able to feed everyone, but we can do something to provide food for someone. Some actions we can take to address this hunger issue include organizing and/or contributing to food drives, making financial donations to organizations who fight against hunger, or volunteering at a local food bank or food pantry.

Let us pray and ask God to show us what we can do to lessen this very serious problem. In doing so, we can make a tangible difference in our communities.

> *If you want to make a difference*
> *in the world, do your part*
> *to feed the hungry!*

DAY 20
REFLECTION TIME

What will you do to address the hunger problem in your city?

_____

_____

_____

_____

_____

_____

_____

_____

_____

_____

_____

Write a prayer asking God to make you more compassionate and sensitive to the needs of those who are hungry.

_____

_____

_____

_____

_____

_____

_____

_____

_____

_____

_____

"Legacy" Devotions

The devotions in this section talk about ways we can make a difference by the legacy we leave.

"We will not hide them from their descendants; we will tell the next generation the praiseworthy deeds of the LORD, his power, and the wonders he has done."

— Psalm 78:4

Day 21
A Life Well-Lived

Read 1 Timothy 4:12–16.

"Don't let anyone look down on you because you are young, but set an example for the believers in speech, in conduct, in love, in faith and in purity."
— 1 Timothy 4:12

*L*egacy can be defined as "something you leave behind or pass on which benefits your family, community, or the world." **Once we believe in Jesus Christ as our Savior and Lord, we can take two actions that will contribute to our Christian legacy: witness about Christ and live for Christ.**

The Day 2 devotion titled "Give Them Jesus" addressed witnessing as a way of showing love to others. The Day 17 and Day 18 devotions titled "The Light of Salvation" talked about witnessing as a way of shining light in the world. **This devotion focuses on witnessing as part of our legacy. After we are gone, someone should be able to say we told others about Christ and encouraged people to believe in Him.**

In our verse for today, the apostle Paul encouraged Timothy to set an example for other believers to follow. **Our example of witnessing for the Lord can motivate other believers to also share their faith in Christ with others.** Ultimately, the more people we can influence to become Christians, either directly through our testimony or indirectly through the witness of those inspired by us, the better the world will be. Why? Because the more sincere and active Christians there are, the more the gospel of Christ will spread. As the gospel spreads and more people believe and embrace it, there will be more committed disciples of Christ who will want to do their part to make a difference in the world.*

In addition to setting an example of witnessing *about* Christ, we should set an example in the way we live *for* Christ. Living a Christlike life can strengthen the faith of other believers, even after we pass away. As a young Christian, I experienced significant spiritual growth from the preaching and teaching of the late Rev. G. V. Clark. I still remember many attributes about his life, including his powerful and encouraging sermons, his faithfulness to God, his activity in the community, his love for people, and his boldness for Christ. **The life he lived for Christ had a tremendous effect on me while he lived and continues even after his death.**

Years after we are no longer here, our dedication and service to the Lord will be remembered and could inspire others to trust in God and live for Him. **Let us strive to serve God the best we can now, so that when our time on this earth is over, we will have left a legacy of a Christian example others will want to emulate.**

If you want to make a difference in the world, leave a legacy of a Christian example!

---

* For assistance in telling others how they can believe in Jesus Christ for salvation, see the section titled "Witnessing About Christ" at the end of this book.

Day 21
Reflection Time

In what ways does your life exhibit Christlike-
ness? In what areas can you improve?

_____

_____

_____

_____

_____

_____

_____

_____

_____

_____

_____

For what acts of love and service will you be remembered?

_____

_____

_____

_____

_____

_____

_____

_____

_____

_____

_____

DAY 22
A LEGACY OF PRAYER

Read Philippians 4:6–8.

"Do not be anxious about anything, but in every situation, by prayer and petition, with thanksgiving, present your requests to God."
– Philippians 4:6

"**P**rayer works." "Prayer changes things." "There is power in prayer." No doubt you have heard these and other sayings about the importance of prayer in the life of a believer. Our focus verse tells us that instead of being anxious about what we are going through, we should take the problem to God in prayer, not only in *some* situations, but in *every* situation.

If we really believe in the power of prayer, we should try to instill that belief in our children and grandchildren. Then when we are no longer here, they will do like us and take everything to the Lord in prayer. We can inspire the younger people in our family to pray in several ways:

- **Teach and encourage them to pray.** If they are young children, teach them Jesus' model prayer (Matthew 6:9–13). As they get older, teach them how to pray to God in their own words. Encourage them to pray to God at all times, both when things are good and when they aren't.

- **Pray with them.** In addition to urging them to pray about what's going on in their lives, we should pray with them. Hearing us pray for their concerns will assist them in learning how to pray better.

- **Let them observe us praying.** Instead of praying privately, we should let our children observe us praying about situations that concern the family. Watching us and listening to our prayers will equip them to be more consistent in praying to God about their problems as they grow older.

- **Tell them how God moved in response to our prayers.** We should tell them that sometimes God answered our prayers like we wanted Him to and sometimes He answered in other ways. However, in either case, God always answered in the way He knew was best. Sharing our experiences of God's responses to our prayers will teach them that prayer is about seeking God's will—not our own.

Even if our children are adults with their own families, it's not too late to exhort them to pray. We can start today and let the younger people in our family know that prayer does work, prayer does change things, and there is power in prayer. In doing so, we will leave a legacy of prayer that others will remember and be inspired by, even after our audible voice can no longer be heard.

If you want to make a difference in the world, be a person of prayer who leaves a legacy of prayer!

DAY 22
REFLECTION TIME

What will you do to encourage other members of your family to pray regularly?

_____

_____

_____

_____

_____

_____

_____

_____

_____

_____

Write some of your prayer requests and how God answered them. Then list the people with whom you will share those answered prayers.

_____

_____

_____

_____

_____

_____

_____

_____

_____

_____

Day 23
Pour into Others

Read Philippians 4:9–13.

"Whatever you have learned or received or heard from me, or seen in me—put it into practice. And the God of peace will be with you."

– Philippians 4:9

*O*ne way we can continue to make a difference in the world after we are gone is to be a mentor. A *mentor* is "someone who nurtures, guides, and enhances the development or growth of another person." **As believers, we should strive to mentor others to live impactful, unselfish, Christlike lives.**

In our focus verse, Paul told the believers at Philippi to take what they had learned from him and put it into practice in their lives. Those believers could not have learned, received, heard, or seen anything from Paul if he had not spent time with them.

From Paul's example, we see that a key to mentoring others is being willing to spend quality time with them. If we plan to mentor others, we must be willing to sacrifice our time to instill Christian teachings, values, and qualities in them. **If we pour into someone else's life and help them develop into a person who makes a difference in the world, then our influence will not end when we die.**

There are three criteria for being an effective mentor:

- **Awareness.** We must be observant so we

can recognize mentoring opportunities. **Mentoring is not always a planned, organized, or formal activity. Sometimes, the opportunity to mentor someone happens spontaneously.**

- **Availability.** We must be ready to take advantage of the opportunities we see to nurture someone. **We shouldn't be so focused on ourselves that we aren't available to participate in the development of others.**

- **Attitude.** We should not look at mentoring as a burden, chore, or inconvenience. **We must have the attitude that mentoring others is a way to make them better**. In addition, we should realize that our mentoring efforts will not only benefit the person we mentor, but they may also impact others whom our mentee may nurture in the future.

Won't you be a spiritual mentor and instill godly values and principles in the people in your sphere of influence?

If you want to make a difference in the world, mentor others to help them grow and develop to be more like Christ!

Day 23
Reflection Time

Who can you mentor in your family, church, or community?

_____

_____

_____

_____

_____

_____

_____

_____

_____

_____

What values and principles will you strive to instill in the persons you mentor?

_____

_____

_____

_____

_____

_____

_____

_____

_____

_____

_____

Day 24
Permanent Inspiration

Read Romans 15:1–4.

"For everything that was written in the past was written to teach us, so that through the endurance taught in the Scriptures and the encouragement they provide we might have hope."
– Romans 15:4

*H*ave you ever wondered how different the world would be if nothing were written down? Writing allows thoughts, actions, and even feelings to be preserved. Writing also gives us an enduring record of valuable, useful, and necessary information.

The most important written work we have is the Bible because it tells us who God is, what He has done for us, how He wants us to live, and how we can live with Him forever. In addition, as our focus verse tells us, the written Scriptures also give us encouragement and hope.

As it relates to legacy, just as the written Word of God provides encouragement, we can leave behind written works that will encourage someone. Writing is permanent. Family and friends may forget what we tell them verbally. Memories of what we said and did may fade as people grow older. However, written words live on long after our verbal words and memories are gone. **That is why writing down our observations, thoughts, and feelings is a great way to leave something that will have a positive, lasting impact on others.**

There are several options for what you can

write to encourage people. **One idea is to write down your favorite Bible passages.** Explain what the verses mean to you and how you are inspired by them. **A Scripture that uplifts and ministers to you may do the same for someone else.**

Another idea is to write letters to your family and friends, telling them everything you want them to know about you, how you feel about them, your prayers for them, etc. Basically, you should include anything you think will be an encouragement to others—both now and after you have passed away.

One last idea is to write a book that will strengthen and build up others. That may sound daunting to some people, but if that is what God leads you to do, He will enable you to do it and give you everything you need to complete the task.

These are just some examples of what you can write to encourage others, but I'm sure you can come up with many more ideas. Please don't underestimate or limit yourself! **You have something inspirational to say that will bless others and make a difference in their lives. Make sure you write it down!**

If you want to make a difference in the world, write something encouraging and share it with others!

DAY 24
REFLECTION TIME

What will you write that can encourage some-one—both now and after you have passed away?

_____

_____

_____

_____

_____

_____

_____

_____

_____

_____

_____

What obstacles might keep you from writing something that will encourage others? How will you overcome those obstacles?

_____

_____

_____

_____

_____

_____

_____

_____

_____

_____

_____

Day 25
Who's Who?

Read Genesis 5:1–14.

"This is the written account of Adam's family line...."

– Genesis 5:1

*A*s we read through the Bible, we encounter numerous genealogies. A *genealogy* is "the history of a family over several generations" and could include births, marriages, names of children, and deaths. Today's reading shows a brief genealogy from Adam through Kenan. To see more of Adam's family line, read the rest of Genesis chapter 5.

A great gift to leave our families is a written record of our ancestors. The fact that God included genealogies in the Bible tells us that family history is important. **The more we know about our ancestors—who they were and how they lived— the greater we will be able to appreciate how God kept our families through the years.**

Unfortunately, many people do not think about recording ancestry information until the elder members of the family who had this knowledge have already passed away. **However, it is never too late to start gathering facts on your family history.** While you might not be able to get all the ancestry data you would like, having some information is better than not having any at all.

Start by asking your oldest living relatives to tell you everything they know about your family's history. In addition to names and dates, also ask for stories of anything your ancestors did that was memorable. If possible, try to find out which ones were Christians and in what ways they served the Lord. **You might find that some of your ancestors have a rich heritage of Christian service.** If the family members with whom you talk don't have all the information you need, they might be able to direct you to someone who can fill in the missing details.

Many services and websites can assist in researching your family members. Some of these websites contain very informative documents, such as census records that not only tell you a person's age, parents, and siblings, but also list their occupations. We might have some personal history data and knowledge that no one else in the extended family has. **Failing to compile this information could mean its loss to future generations. That is why recording whatever family data we can before our last grain of sand drops and our life ends is so important!**

After you have completed your research and collected as much information as you can, pass your records on to the younger members of the family. Encourage them to continue recording the family history and keep the records current and up-to-date. **Passing down your family history is a great legacy to leave, and your loved ones will appreciate you taking the time to preserve this valuable information.**

If you want to make a difference in the world, document your family's history and pass it on to the younger generations!

Day 25
Reflection Time

With which of your family members will you talk to gather information about your ancestors?

_____

_____

_____

_____

_____

_____

_____

_____

_____

_____

Search the Internet to find genealogy websites, and list the ones you plan to consult to assist you in researching your family history.

_____

_____

_____

_____

_____

_____

_____

_____

_____

_____

DAY 26
DON'T KEEP IT TO YOURSELF

Read Psalm 78:1–7.

"We will not hide them from their descendants; we will tell the next generation the praiseworthy deeds of the LORD, his power, and the wonders he has done."

– Psalm 78:4

A *testimony* is "a spoken statement of something a person has seen or experienced." Testimonies are important in a court of law when deciding a defendant's innocence or guilt. Testimonies are also valuable in letting others know what God has done for us. **However, a testimony is only helpful when it is shared. All of us should be able to testify to "the praiseworthy deeds of the LORD, his power, and the wonders he has done" in our lives.**

Today's focus verse lets us know we should not hide what God did for us from our descendants. **Psalm 78:6–7 tell us why we should tell young people what God has done for us:**

- **"So the next generation would know"** (v. 6). How can the next generations know what God has done if we hide it from them? We should think back over all the Lord has done for us over the course of our life and make it a point to share those stories with the younger generations every opportunity we get. **Telling young people what God did for us could make a huge difference in how they live.**

- **"They in turn would tell their children"** (v. 6). Firsthand accounts of God's demonstration of His power in our lives are the most effective. After we are dead and gone, someone may tell our children and grandchildren what God did for us, **but no one can give our testimonies better than we can.** As we tell the younger generations what God has done for us, we should encourage them to share these stories with their children.

- **"Then they would put their trust in God"** (v. 7). The more we testify to young people about God's activity in our life, the more they will have to remember, draw upon, and apply to their lives. **Ultimately, our testimonies of what God did for us will strengthen the faith of younger generations and inspire them to trust God more.**

Let us not take our testimonies of God's goodness to the grave with us. **Instead, let's share them with others, especially younger people, as often as we can.**

If you want to make a difference in the world, share the testimonies of God's goodness in your life with others!

DAY 26
REFLECTION TIME

What "praiseworthy deeds" has God performed in your life that you can share with others?

_____

_____

_____

_____

_____

_____

_____

_____

_____

_____

_____

Make a list of the people with whom you will share your testimonies of God's goodness, then make sure you tell them.

_____

_____

_____

_____

_____

_____

_____

_____

_____

_____

_____

Day 27
What Do These Stones Mean?

Read Joshua 4:1–9, 20–24.

"... These stones are to be a memorial to the people of Israel forever."

– Joshua 4:7

A memorial is "an object or place that is designed to preserve the memory of a person or event." Some popular forms of memorials include landmarks, parks, statues, fountains, and monuments. We see memorials in many cities around the world.

However, in today's story we see a different type of memorial. In Joshua chapter 3, God parted the Jordan River to allow the Israelites to cross. In Joshua chapter 4, God commanded Joshua to choose twelve men, one from each tribe, and tell them to take up twelve stones from the middle of the Jordan River. These stones were to serve as memorials to remind the Israelites' descendants that God performed a mighty miracle to allow His people to cross over the Jordan on dry ground. **So even when the people who actually crossed the Jordan were no longer around, the stones would remind the people what God did for their ancestors and inspire them to put their trust in that same God.**

We can similarly impact future generations by leaving some kind of memorial to our family to remind them of our faith in God and our dedication to Him. Leaving a physical memorial would be a constant, visible reminder to our loved ones of our walk with God and would encourage them to follow our example of serving the Lord.

One memorial we could leave is our Bible, which would be symbolic of the life we lived for Christ. That Bible would be especially meaningful if some of our favorite Scriptures were highlighted or if it contained handwritten sermon notes. I was an adult when my maternal grandmother passed away, and my uncle gave my grandmother's Bible to me. I always thought that Bible was simply a good keepsake by which I could remember my grandmother. However, in the process of writing this devotion, I now realize I have a treasure that represents a legacy of faith existing in my family at least two generations before me! Other examples of a memorial could be a piece of jewelry, like a necklace with a cross, or even an article of clothing. **Try to choose a memorial that will motivate future generations to trust God and follow Him wholeheartedly, as you endeavored to do.**

Joshua told the Israelites to explain the meaning of the stone memorials to their children so their descendants would know what the stones represent. **Likewise, your memorial will be more impactful if you show your family what you are leaving them, tell them why you are leaving it, and explain its significance.** What kind of memorial will *you* leave? Be creative!

If you want to make a difference in the world, leave a memorial that will remind others of your devotion to Jesus Christ and encourage them to follow the Lord!

DAY 27
REFLECTION TIME

What memorials can you leave your family?

_____

_____

_____

_____

_____

_____

_____

_____

_____

_____

_____

_____

What message of God's grace and power do you want your memorials to convey to your family?

_____

_____

_____

_____

_____

_____

_____

_____

_____

_____

_____

DAY 28
TEACHABLE MOMENTS

Read Deuteronomy 6:1–9.

"Impress them on your children. Talk about them when you sit at home and when you walk along the road, when you lie down and when you get up."
– Deuteronomy 6:7

I thank God for the many dedicated Sunday school teachers, Vacation Bible school teachers, and youth ministry workers who are so instrumental in teaching children about God. **However, children spend more time with their parents than they do with teachers at church, so parents must still do their part to teach their children who God is, what He has done, and how He wants them to live.**

We see the importance of parents teaching their children in today's reading, where Moses instructed the Israelites to teach the commandments of God to their children. He said they should talk to their children about God's Word when they are at home, when they are not at home, before they go to bed, and after they wake up in the morning. In other words, they were to talk with their children about God every chance they got. What great advice for us today! **We should take advantage of every opportunity we get to talk with our children about God.** Deuteronomy 6:2 tells us why teaching our children God's Word is so important: so they and their children will reverence the Lord and keep His commands as long as they live.

In addition to talking about God with our

children, we should also talk about Him to our nieces, nephews, cousins, and any other young family members who we can influence for the Lord. Even more, we should not only talk with the younger people in our families when they are children. We must continue to speak the Word of God to our family members even after they become adults.

If we do our job and plant the Word of God in our younger family members, those teachings will take root, blossom in them, and help them become the Christians God wants them to be. Proverbs 22:6 tells us, *"Start children off on the way they should go, and even when they are old they will not turn from it."*

Once our children are grown and we are no longer here, they will remember what they were taught and will teach the Word of God to their children, who prayerfully will teach it to their children, and so on. Raising young people who love God and obey His Word is a great legacy to leave after we are gone.

If you want to make a difference in the world, teach your children and other young people in your family the Word of God!

DAY 28
REFLECTION TIME

What steps will you take to actively teach the young people in your family about God?

_____

_____

_____

_____

_____

_____

_____

_____

_____

_____

_____

Write a prayer asking God to help you teach your children and other younger family members what the Bible says.

_____

_____

_____

_____

_____

_____

_____

_____

_____

_____

_____

Day 29
Write It Down

Read Exodus 17:8–16.

"... Write this on a scroll as something to be re-membered and make sure that Joshua hears it ..."
– Exodus 17:14

Many people keep a journal documenting their thoughts, actions, experiences, observations, and feelings. **Some people may journal daily, while others journal only when they want to capture some notable event that occurred.**

Recording what happened so it can be preserved is not new. Several times in the Bible God told someone to write something down for various reasons. In today's focus verse, God told Moses to write down how He had given Joshua and the Israelites the victory over the Amalekites because He said it was "something to be remembered."

Many events happen in our lives that would be good for us to remember, and journaling gives us a way to document those moments. Journaling serves the following purposes:

- **Enables us to observe how God covered, kept, and blessed us throughout our lives.**

- **Allows us to look back over our lives and see how we grew spiritually over the years.**

- **Strengthens us to face problems in the present because we can reflect on how God delivered us in the past.**

- **Reminds us of how God answered our prayers.**

- **Shows us how God kept His promises.**

Our journal, which benefits us, can also help other people if we share what we have written with them. Notice that in addition to telling Moses to write down what happened, God told him to "make sure that Joshua hears it." **From a legacy perspective, keeping a journal and passing it on to our children and family members will give them a front row seat into our day-to-day walk with God.** Our descendants will be able to see some of the challenges we faced, how we took our problems to God in prayer, how the Lord fortified us, and how He brought us through our troubles. **As they read through the pages of our journal, future generations will see how we trusted in God, and they will be inspired to do the same.**

Many examples of how to depend on God in difficult times can be learned from our lives. Keeping a journal is a good way to leave these lessons so others can profit from them. We never know how our experiences with the Lord will encourage and minister to others. **Even though journaling requires work, it is worthwhile because our journal could have a significant and lasting effect on those who read it.**

If you want to make a difference in the world, keep a journal and pass it on!

DAY 29
REFLECTION TIME

If you journal now, why did you start? If you don't journal, what is stopping you from starting today?

_____

_____

_____

_____

_____

_____

_____

_____

_____

_____

_____

How will you ensure your journal is handed down to your loved ones when you pass away?

_____

_____

_____

_____

_____

_____

_____

_____

_____

_____

_____

Day 30
A Legacy of Presence

Read Philippians 1:1–11.

"I thank my God every time I remember you."
– Philippians 1:3

*L*eaving a "legacy of presence" means being active, involved, and present in the lives of our family and friends right now, while we still have grains of sand remaining in our life's hourglass.

Paul told the Philippian Christians that he thanked God every time he remembered them. Paul had vivid memories of these believers' "partnership in the gospel" (v. 5). **If we want to be remembered by others, we must spend time with them making memories.** When we die, the memories of all that we did with our family members could make coping with our passing a little easier.

In 1984 I went to spend a week with my paternal grandmother in Savannah, Georgia. We had a great time talking, laughing, and just being with each other. A month after I returned home to Austin, Texas, I received word from my dad that my grandmother had passed away. During her funeral, I actually had a smile on my face because of the memories of the enjoyable time I had with her a month earlier. I would not have had those wonderful memories of my grandmother if I had not taken the time to spend that week with her.

One day, we will no longer be here; we will be with the Lord in heaven. That is why making the sacrifices necessary to spend as much time

with our family and friends as we can is so important. We should try to take as many pictures and videos as we can of our time with others. After we are gone, those pictures and videos will allow them to look back and reminisce about the happy times they had with us.

Even without the benefit of pictures and videos, our loved ones can still recall the time they spent with us through the power of memories. One of the most amazing capabilities of the human brain is its ability to retain memories. Our brains allow us to recall what happened decades ago as well as remembering what we did this morning. **We must seek to be present in the lives of our family and friends, so we can make memories that outlive us.** Take the time to leave a legacy of presence; you won't regret it.

If you want to make a difference in the world, make time to be present in the lives of your loved ones and create memories!

DAY 30
REFLECTION TIME

What will you do to make it a priority to spend more time with family and friends?

_____

_____

_____

_____

_____

_____

_____

_____

_____

_____

_____

With whom is the Holy Spirit prompting you to spend time?

_____

_____

_____

_____

_____

_____

_____

_____

_____

_____

Conclusion

I pray that the devotions you read in this book have given you a stronger desire to make a difference in the world. God did not put us here only for ourselves. We were created to be social beings who interact with others. **Every day we live, God gives us an opportunity to be a positive influence on the lives of the people around us.**

Please keep this devotional in a place where it will be a constant reminder to look for ways you can make a difference. **Periodically reread your journal responses and prayers to remind yourself what you said you would do and what you asked God to do.**

I want to warn us that two types of attitudes will keep us from making a difference: selfishness and procrastination. Having an attitude of selfishness will lead us to choose to do something for ourselves instead of someone else. However, if we are unselfish, we will do what we can to assist others. We know God wants us to be unselfish because Philippians 2:4 tells us, *"Not looking to your own interests but each of you to the interests of the others."*

Procrastination is "the act of putting off, delaying, or postponing something." In John 9:4, Jesus said, *"As long as it is day, we must do the works of him who sent me. Night is coming, when no one can work."* With regard to procrastination, this verse says we must do what we need to do while we have time to do it. **When we procrastinate, we decide against doing something now, while telling ourselves we will do it later. The danger with procrastination is that "later" may never come**.

We might completely forget about that task and never do it, or we may not get another chance to do it. **Either way, we may have let an opportunity to bless someone slip away and that chance might never come again.**

Let us ask God to help us guard against selfishness and procrastination so we can take advantage of the time He gives us to make a difference in someone's life. **Every day you live, I encourage you to make the world better by showing love to others, being a light to everyone with whom you come in contact, and leaving a legacy that will live on after you are gone.**

Every second you live you have one less grain of sand in your life's hourglass. When that last grain of sand drops and your life on this side is over, what will you have done to uplift someone, brighten someone's life, and make the world a better place? Will God be pleased with how you let your light shine? Remember the story of the starfish? **You can't help everybody, but through God's power, you can make somebody's life better. Won't you do what you can to change the world and make a difference while you have time?**

WITNESSING ABOUT CHRIST

*M*any methods can be used to witness to others about Jesus Christ. **Regardless of which method is used, if we are going to be effective witnesses, we must depend on the power of the Holy Spirit and follow His leading.** In Acts 1:8, Jesus said, *"But you will receive power when the Holy Spirit comes on you; and you will be my witnesses in Jerusalem, and in all Judea and Samaria, and to the ends of the earth."*

One approach to witnessing about the good news of Jesus Christ is called the "Romans Road to Salvation." This approach uses verses from the book of Romans to explain why we need salvation, how God provided salvation, how we can receive salvation, and the results of salvation. There are several variations of the "Romans Road" and they all may not reference the same scriptures. But the good news is that all of the Romans Road versions lead to the same destination—salvation through faith in Jesus Christ!

If possible, have the person you are witnessing to read the verses for themselves. That will let them know that what you are telling them about being saved comes from God, not you. I pray that these verses will be helpful as you communicate the truth of the gospel of Jesus Christ to others.

1. **Romans 3:23** – *"For all have sinned and fall short of the glory of God."* We all have done something that was against God's commands.

2. **Romans 6:23** – *"For the wages of sin is death, but the gift of God is eternal life in*

Christ Jesus our Lord." The Bible tells us that the result of the sins we commit is spiritual death, which is a broken relationship with God and separation from Him. However, through belief in Jesus Christ, instead of spiritual death, God gave us the gift of eternal life, meaning we can live with Him forever.

3. **Romans 5:8** – *"But God demonstrates his own love for us in this: While we were still sinners, Christ died for us."* Because of God's great love for us, He sent His Son, Jesus Christ, to pay the penalty for our sins. Jesus was crucified on the cross and died in our place.

4. **Romans 10:9–10** – *"If you declare with your mouth, 'Jesus is Lord,' and believe in your heart that God raised him from the dead, you will be saved. For it is with your heart that you believe and are justified, and it is with your mouth that you profess your faith and are saved."* Whoever acknowledges that Jesus is Lord and believes in their heart that God raised Him from the dead has the assurance from God that they are saved and have eternal life.

5. **Romans 5:1** – *"Therefore, since we have been justified through faith, we have peace with God through our Lord Jesus Christ."* One of the results of our salvation is that we have peace with God. We are no longer separated from God because Jesus' death paid the penalty for our sins.

6. **Romans 8:1** – *"Therefore, there is now no condemnation for those who are in Christ Jesus."* Another result of our salvation is that we are no longer and never will be condemned by God because we placed our faith in Jesus Christ.

After you have shared these verses with the person, ask them if they would like to believe in Jesus and accept the free gift of eternal life that God offers them. If they say they want to believe in Jesus, have them repeat a prayer similar to the following:

"God, I know that I have sinned against you. I am sorry for what I have done and ask you to forgive me. I believe that Jesus Christ is Lord, He died on the cross for my sins, and you raised Him from the dead. I put my faith in Jesus Christ as my Savior. Thank you for saving me and giving me eternal life. In Jesus' name, I pray. Amen!"

Let them know that the words themselves are not what saves them. Salvation comes only by faith in Jesus Christ. This prayer is their verbal confession that they believe what Jesus did to provide salvation for them.

Putting their faith in Jesus Christ is just the beginning of the person's new life with the Lord. Encourage them to join a church where they can worship God with other believers. Ask them to attend corporate Bible study. Teach them how to pray and study the Bible for themself.

Author Information

1. Email address: japerrysr@gmail.com
2. Website: https://joeyaperry.com
3. Blog: https://joeyaperry.com/blog
4. Social media:
   - Twitter: @japerry2000 (https://twitter.com/japerry2000)
   - LinkedIn: Joey Perry (https://www.linkedin.com/in/joey-perry-9295174/)
   - Instagram: Joey Perry (https://www.instagram.com/japerryfwd/)
   - Facebook: Joey A. Perry Sr., Author (https://www.facebook.com/japerrysr)
5. Other books by this author (available on Amazon):
   - *Parenting Lessons from God, the Perfect Parent*
   - *Pressing on Toward Maturity: Seven Biblical Truths for Spiritual Growth*
   - *One Less Grain of Sand: Fulfill God's Purposes While You Have Time!*
6. Reviews are very important to authors! Please consider leaving a review.